Sticky

How to Deal with Life

Brandon Russell

Table of Contents

INTRODUCTION

Before We Begin

I'm not a psychologist or a therapist. But I've been a coach most of my life. I'm a dad, an uncle, a brother, a teacher, and a husband. I met Sticky as a relatively young man, and he's helped me through more situations than I can count. He doesn't have an answer for everything, and honestly, not everything has an answer. But looking back on what I've learned working with Sticky, I believe others might benefit from his approach. It's not foolproof. But it is practical. And sometimes, that's enough to keep moving.

So without further ado…

Meet Sticky

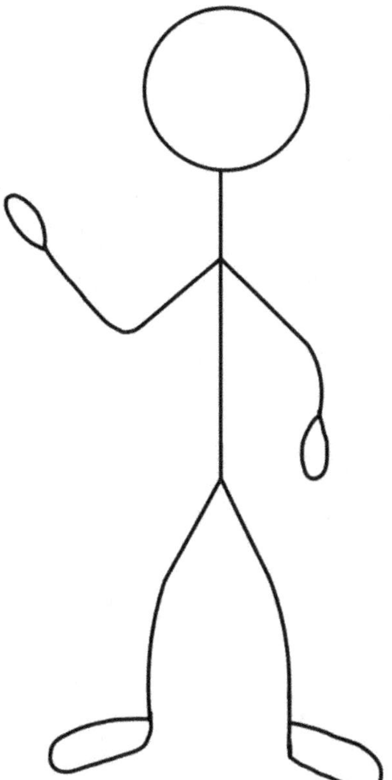

Let me introduce you to Sticky.

Sticky is a stick figure. A simple little guy just trying to get through life. He's not special. He's not enlightened. He just keeps finding himself in sticky situations. And honestly? He reminds me a lot of me. When I was a young football player in high school, we had a team manager who kept popping a few of us with a towel in the locker room. The first few times, I ignored it. I was tired from practice, stressed about life at home, and didn't want to make it a thing. So I let it go. But he didn't stop. Over and over, he kept doing it. And I kept swallowing it. Then one day, I snapped. I exploded. We fought right there in the locker room. And it wasn't really about the towel. It was about everything I hadn't dealt with. The exhaustion. The pressure. The tension I was carrying. That towel was just the last thing to hit me. Years later, the scene looked different. But the story hadn't changed much.

It was a Sunday morning. We were running late for church. My wife and I hadn't been married long. My two small kids were making everything harder, not easier. And the dog, Charlie, had made a disaster in the backyard. When I went to bring him inside, he knew he was in trouble. He ducked behind a bench by the door. I lost it. I grabbed the bench and threw it across the yard. I yanked Charlie up by the scruff of his neck and shoved him inside. Then I turned around and saw the look on my family's faces. Silent. Stunned. Afraid. Nobody said a word on the way to church. I tell you this because we all have our versions of that Sunday morning, or that locker room. Moments when the small stuff hits a raw nerve. When we hold things in until we break. When we pretend we're fine, until we're not. That's where Sticky lives.

Sticky might look different than you. His story may not match yours exactly. But the feelings, the weight, the silence, that part belongs to all of us. Sticky has tools, as do you. We are going to learn what those are and how to use them.

Let's figure it out together, you, me, and Sticky.

"If any of you lacks wisdom, let him ask God, who gives generously to all without reproach, and it will be given him." James 1:5

Life Fires the Cannon
When It All Hits at Once

Life doesn't ask permission before it fires. It doesn't wait for a good time, or check to see if you've been doing everything right. You can be loving your family, serving your community, showing up for people, none of that puts you off-limits. When life decides to launch a cannonball your way, you're getting hit. Sometimes it's small stuff: little annoyances, unexpected interruptions, daily frustrations. But other times, it feels like a full cannon barrage, one hit after another before you've had a chance to recover from the last one. That's what started happening to Sticky.

He was just trying to get through his day, doing good things, holding it together, giving his best to the people around him. And then the cannon fired. And fired again. And again. At first, he thought he could take it. Just another hit. Just another day. But the pace picked up. There was no time to catch his breath, no space to think. Just noise, smoke, and incoming fire. Sticky wasn't dodging anymore. He was getting buried. And I've been there.

Not long before Sticky came into my life, I was in what looked like a good season. My family was in a strong place. I was making more money than ever before. I was involved at church, and I was coaching high school students and mentoring them. It felt like we were doing everything right. Then the cannon fired.

Our pastor resigned, and I was told I would need to resign too. Half our income disappeared overnight. The very next day, our landlord told us the house we were renting had been sold. We had to move. No warning, no backup plan. Then came the flat tire, the pressure from student loans, the custody issues, the emotional stress, the financial fear. It all came at once, and it didn't stop. I couldn't sleep without medication. One morning at school, I almost fainted. They loaded me into an ambulance. My blood pressure had spiked. My body just couldn't keep up anymore. It wasn't one bad moment. It was the entire load. One cannonball after another. And it was too much. That's exactly where Sticky was, buried under hit after hit with no time to breathe.

That's how it happens for most people. Not necessarily because of one huge traumatic event, but because of accumulation. The stacking. The slow build. The feeling that you've been carrying too much for too long, and one more hit might break you. It's why people explode. It's why they shut down or walk away from jobs, relationships, communities, anything they once cared about. Because life rarely throws just one thing at you. It loads the cannon with five or ten, and fires them all at once.

That is what this is about: recognizing that moment. The point when the hits aren't just random stress, they're starting to take you out. If you don't know you're under fire, you won't know how close you are to breaking. Sticky didn't know. But that was about to change.

"In the world you will have tribulation. But take heart; I have overcome the world."
John 16:33

The Shield

The Art of Not Dealing With It, Until You Have To

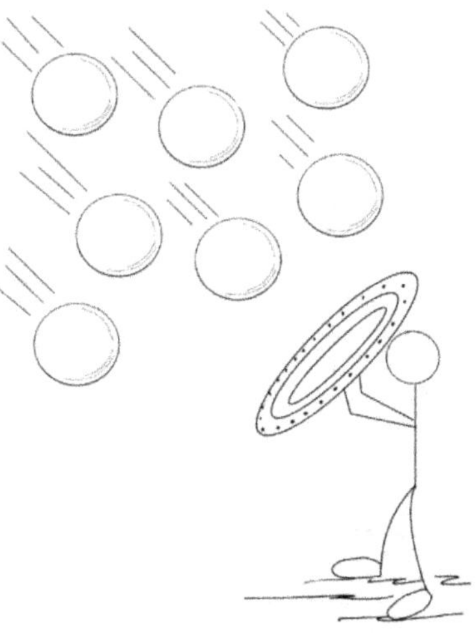

Sticky didn't fall apart all at once. He held it together for a while. Every time life fired another cannonball, he raised his shield. He did what most of us do: he blocked it, brushed it off, smiled through it, and kept going. And for a while, it worked. Sort of. The shield didn't solve anything, but it bought time. It made him look strong. It helped him avoid hard conversations. It gave him a moment to breathe without breaking.

The shield isn't a solution. It's a survival mechanism. And survival isn't healing.

The shield takes different forms. For some, it's humor. For others, productivity—staying busy, staying sharp, staying ahead of the emotions. Sometimes it's avoidance: a drink, a scroll, a screen. Sometimes it's silence. Shut it down. Don't let it in.

And often, the shield looks like blame. If someone else is at fault, then we get to stay safe behind the illusion that we're in control. If I'm just reacting to what life is doing to me, I don't have to examine what I'm carrying or how I'm responding. Blame becomes a convenient buffer between discomfort and growth.

Sticky's shield got a workout. Stress, rejection, disappointment, burnout—he had a defense for all of it. And to be fair, it helped. But over time, it started doing damage of its own. Because life kept firing. And the shield didn't get stronger. It got heavier.

Eventually, Sticky wasn't just holding the shield. He was hiding behind it. And without noticing it, he began to fade.

Just days before I ended up in an ambulance, I was walking through the halls of a high school. I was laughing with teachers, meeting with the principal, leading prayer groups with students. I was helping kids. Helping the school. Helping everybody.

By all outward appearances, life was good. I had great kids. A strong marriage. A job I loved. I looked good. I sounded good. I was doing everything I was supposed to be doing.

And I told myself I was fine.

The things bothering me? Just stress. Just minor stuff. Inconveniences. Like a small hit, you feel it, but it's just annoying. Something you push past without a second thought. But day after day, the little things add up. And eventually, they stop being small. Because when you never deal with the small stuff, it doesn't stay small.

So when they loaded me into that ambulance, it was obvious, to me and to everyone else, I was not okay. Sticky was in that same place, holding the shield up until he couldn't anymore.

That wasn't a crack. That was the moment the shield finally slipped out of my hands. I had nothing left to grip it with. My mind was full. My body was tired. I was at the bottom of a pile of things I'd been pretending weren't heavy. That's what the shield does. It lets us play the part. It buys us time. But it doesn't process pain. It doesn't remove stress. It doesn't heal a thing.

Eventually, if you never stop to deal with what's really going on, the shield becomes too heavy to hold. And the stuff you were trying to keep out? It finds its way in any way.

Sticky didn't lay the shield down. He didn't make a decision to face the hard stuff. He simply couldn't hold it anymore. And when the weight finally overtook him, he realized the shield hadn't failed.

It had done exactly what it was meant to do. It just couldn't do it forever.

"But he said to me, 'My grace is sufficient for you, for my power is made perfect in weakness.'"
2 Corinthians 12:9

The Ball Itself

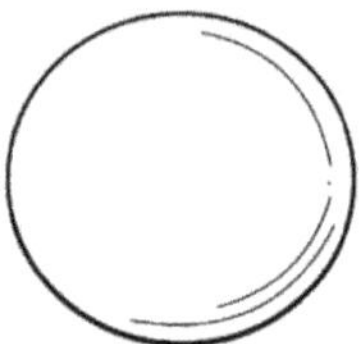

What's really inside the stuff that buries us?

Sticky had been hit. Hard. Repeatedly. And at some point, he stopped asking why and just focused on bracing for the next shot.

Some cannonballs are obvious, big, heavy, life-changing even. Others hit out of nowhere. They're never quite the same in size or shape. Trust me though, they all hurt. And what hurts most isn't always the impact. It's what they really mean.

One day Sticky stopped and picked up one of the cannonballs that had knocked him over. Just out of curiosity. And he realized it wasn't what he expected. It was soft. Wrapped. Sealed in tight layers like plastic wrap. You could barely see inside it, let alone understand it.

These are the hits we don't fully process. The vague stuff. The things that bothered us, but we never slowed down long enough to name them. Maybe it was a word someone said or a moment that felt off, but we shrugged it off and kept moving. So the pain stayed wrapped. And the longer it stayed unspoken, the harder it became to name.

Some cannonballs don't look dangerous at all. From the outside, they seem harmless. Maybe even good. They don't feel like something that should knock you down.

So back to Sticky. He's going through the pile, picks up a ball, and breaks it open. This one looked bright and harmless on the outside, even sweet. But once he broke it open, the smell hit him. It had rotted from the inside. This one was deceptive. A hit he thought was good for him, even healthy. Maybe it was a job opportunity. A relationship. A cause. But over time, it had turned. What once felt sweet had become toxic, and he was still carrying it like it was a gift.

And then sometimes, the hit isn't massive. It's not a full-body takedown. It doesn't knock you down. But it still hits. Quick. Sharp. Unexpected. I had one of those recently. I was just scrolling Facebook, not really looking for anything, when I saw a post about something from my past. A memory. A connection.

Something that had once been mine, but was no longer. That's all it took. One glance. One post. And impact.

It wasn't catastrophic. It didn't wreck my day. But it hit something tender. I felt it. Hurt, shame, a little anger. It was judgment aimed at who I used to be, landing on who I've become.

In that moment, I had a choice. Not a dramatic, life-changing one. Just a quiet one. I could absorb it. React to it. Let it spiral.

Or I could look at it. Name it. Forgive it. And keep going.

That's what I did. I didn't shove it down. I didn't pretend it didn't sting. I just saw it for what it was: a fresh hit thrown at an old version of me. And it didn't need to stay with me.

Those are real too. The quiet hits. The unexpected reminders. The small hits. They don't bury you, but they still count. Especially when you deal with them instead of letting them define you.

There was another kind of cannonball that Sticky found. This one was solid. Rough. Heavy. No wrapping. No disguise. Just weight. But when he broke it open, something glimmered inside. A gem. Something beautiful. Something shaped by pressure.

This kind of hit changes you. It breaks something open and reveals a piece of who you're becoming. You wouldn't have chosen it. You wouldn't want to go through it again. But looking back, you see what it made possible. The wisdom. The clarity. The strength.

Sticky started to realize not every hit was meant to destroy him. Some were meant to wake him up.

And maybe that's where it starts. Not with getting better. Not with fixing everything. Just picking up one ball. Looking at it. Asking what it really is. And deciding that maybe not all of it needs to be carried anymore.

That's what we'll do next: we'll start to sort the pile.

"Count it all joy, my brothers, when you meet trials of various kinds, for you know that the testing of your faith produces steadfastness." James 1:2–3

The Pile-Up
It's Not Just What Life Throws, It's What You Don't Deal With

When Sticky dropped the shield, the hits didn't stop. The cannonballs kept coming. And now, without anything to deflect them, they started to stack. First one, then another. Then five more. They landed and rolled and piled until Sticky was no longer just under pressure. He was under everything.

That's how it happens. Not all at once. Not always with some massive trauma or big, dramatic life failure. Most of the time? It starts with small things.

Unpaid tolls. A $5 fee turns into a $50 fine just because you didn't open the envelope. A paper cut. You ignore it. Don't clean it. And now it's red and swollen and aching because you didn't think something that small could cause that much trouble. Little things, when ignored, start to stack. And eventually, that can crush you.

It's not just the big things. It's the stack of stuff we ignored, because each hit felt so small.

Let me tell you a story. Names have been changed to protect the innocent, and the chronically over-optimistic.

Meet Sarah.

Sarah had a gift: she could accumulate things like it was a quiet superpower. Not on purpose, it just… happened. A magazine left on the coffee table. A sweater casually draped over the back of a chair. Then another sweater. Then three more. Soon, the chair wasn't really a chair anymore. It was more like a wool-covered mountain silently daring anyone to sit on it.

Her husband, Mark, was a "place for everything, everything in its place" type of guy. He watched the slow progression with quiet dread and the occasional passive-aggressive attempt to "clear a path."

Then came the morning he woke up and realized Sarah's side of the bed was several inches higher than his. Why? Because somewhere in the night, a mountain of clean laundry had migrated from the floor to the bed. It wasn't folded. It wasn't even sorted. But it was stacked, and it was winning.

"Morning, Mount Washmore," he mumbled.

But the true breaking point was the kitchen. Sarah loved to cook, but had a habit of "leaving ingredients out for later." One morning, Mark nudged a lone spatula that had been sitting on the counter since Tuesday, and that was it. The spatula tipped over a stack of takeout menus. The menus knocked over an open bag of flour. The flour exploded. The flour hit the onion. The onion rolled through a spilled box of cereal. And just like that, their kitchen looked like it had been hit by a snowstorm and a cooking show at the same time.

Mark stood there in silence, holding a single cup of coffee. Sarah walked in, surveyed the damage, and burst out laughing.

"Well," she said, "at least we know where the thyme went. It's probably somewhere under the Frosted Flakes."

That's the pile. Not always catastrophic. Not always loud. But left unchecked? It builds. And even if it's slow, even if it's soft, it crashes. Sticky had been living under that same kind of pile, only his wasn't funny. And for some people, it doesn't stay manageable for long. Sometimes you don't even know you're under it until someone asks, "Are you okay?" and you can't answer without crying or lying. Sometimes your body breaks before your voice does. Sometimes you're so used to the weight, you forget what it's like to stand up straight. But the pile lets you know it's there.

It shows up in irritability, fatigue, anxiety, silence, anger, overreactions, withdrawal. It leaks into your relationships. It eats up your margin. It makes you feel like you're constantly behind, like something's wrong but you can't name it.

That's the pile. And if you don't do something with it, it will do something with you.

Sticky had lost his footing. He'd dropped his precious shield. Now, there's more stuff than Sticky. Now he has to make a decision. What can he possibly do under so much weight? The weight of life's bangers that have knocked him down, ones he refused to deal with. His decision is coming. And when it does, you'll see what he chose, and how you can choose too. It's easy to laugh with Sarah and Mark because their pile was visible. You can see flour on an onion. You can sweep up the Frosted Flakes.

But what happens when the mess is invisible? What happens when the weight you're carrying isn't made of clean laundry, but of the silent hits you've spent years pretending aren't heavy?

For Sticky, the "funny" pile was over. He was stepping into a different kind of room. The kind that doesn't just ruin a kitchen. It threatens to ruin a life.

Before we look at how he got out, we have to acknowledge how dark it can get when the weight becomes more than a person can carry. Because for some, the pile isn't something you laugh about later. It's the moment the weight finally forces a choice. And in that moment, the pressure doesn't feel temporary. It feels permanent.

"Come to me, all you who are weary and burdened, and I will give you rest."
Matthew 11:28

The Choice Point
When It's Too Much

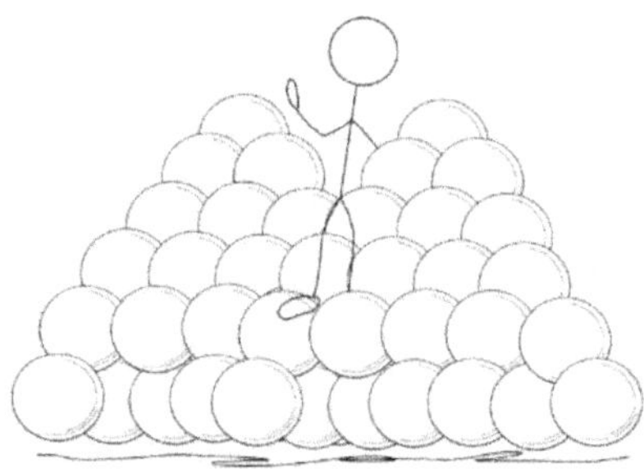

Sticky never planned to end up here. One day, he was functioning, maybe even thriving. And the next? He was buried. Exhausted. Silent. The shield was gone. The cannonballs had landed. And everything was still firing, even as he sat still under the weight.

That's how it works. You don't notice how heavy life is getting until your arms won't move, your breath is short, and your eyes are full of tears you didn't expect.

Then comes the moment. The tipping point. The point where you no longer feel like you're carrying something. You feel crushed.

You're standing in your kitchen at 7 a.m., trying to get your kids dressed while emails blow up your phone, and the dog throws up on the carpet. You're holding it together at work until someone makes a joke in a meeting and your hands are shaking under the table.

I'm fine. I'm fine. I'm fine.

Suddenly, I'm screaming in traffic, or curled up in the bathroom, or punching the steering wheel, or whispering, "I can't do this anymore," to a room with nobody in it.

That's the moment. Not rage. Not despair. Just overload.

It's too much.

This is what I call the Choice Point.

Only, it doesn't feel like a choice. It feels like you've run out of them.

And your brain starts offering up the only exits it can find.

And for some people, this moment doesn't just feel overwhelming.

It feels like there are only a few ways out, and none of them are good.

Some people explode.

They blow up, yell, slam, throw, lash out, detach, or do something reckless just to feel something. But when you explode from under the pile, it doesn't just clear your mess. It sends pieces of it flying onto everyone around you. Shrapnel hits your family. Your friends. Your team. Your kids. And it leaves a crater underneath you. You lose ground, trust, connection. And most of the time, the pile is still there. Just rearranged.

Others quit. Not always in a loud way. Sometimes it's soft. You pull back. You shut down. You stop talking. You stop trying. And sometimes it's darker. For some, "quit" means leaving a marriage, walking off the job, walking out of their life. For others, it means ending their life altogether. Because the pain of being buried feels permanent. And suicide can look like the only way to make the pain stop.

But that decision, the most final version of "I'm done," doesn't take away the pile. It just passes it on to the people who loved you most. The ones who now carry what you couldn't. Now they carry the loss of you, and that is crushing all by itself.

That's not judgment. That's heartbreak.

I know because I've had a loved one take their own life. That is a wrecking ball.

And if you're reading this and you've felt it, really felt it, I want you to know something:

You are not weak for wanting it to end. You are not crazy for feeling buried. But quitting isn't your only option.

That's the third path. The real one. The one that changes everything.

Sticky sat in that tension. He didn't want to explode. He didn't want to quit. But he didn't know what else to do, until something inside him said, "Look at that stuff. What is it really?"

16

And maybe, so have you.

You might not look like him. Your story might be different. But the pressure, the silence, the not knowing what to do, that connects us. This is the "take control of my life" path. The moment you stop reacting and start responding. Not in a "Just get over it" way. Not in a "You deal with it" finger-pointing way. But by actually looking at the stuff life has thrown at you.

It's the quiet way forward. The one we don't see until we are still, or even broken enough, to stop dodging and start seeing. To realize, "I'm not just under pressure. I'm under stuff." And maybe, if I could name it, I could sort it.

And that's where everything began to shift.

"The Lord is near to the brokenhearted and saves the crushed in spirit."
Psalm 34:18

Looking at the Stuff
What You're Under Isn't All Junk

Sticky didn't start clawing at the pile with a plan. He just knew he couldn't stay buried. So he reached for the closest thing he could touch, expecting to find a mess of broken memories and useless fragments. But what he found was stranger.

The pile wasn't just chaos. It was a 3D puzzle. Not flat. Not simple. Pieces connected in weird, unexpected ways, some jammed together, some inside others. Sticky breaks one open and finds another. Then another. Until all that's left is a small, almost insignificant ball at the center.

And once Sticky slowed down enough to really look at it, he noticed something else. Some of the cannonballs were the same.

Not exact copies. But close. Same argument with different people. Same emotion wearing a new face. Same fear disguised as a new situation. The layers had changed. But the cores were familiar. Sticky had seen those before.

And here is the wild part. Once he actually dealt with one, once he cracked it open and processed what was really in it, the rest started to dissolve like sand slipping through his fingers.

Sticky dealt with one ball of stuff. Then he looked down and saw where others had been, nothing but sand.

That is what happens when you finally face something you have been dodging for years. It shrinks. And what once felt crushing starts to crumble.

I remember when I first started giving gifts to my brother. He was a carpenter, sharp, skilled, no nonsense. I loved getting him little things he could use, but I also loved messing with him. So I would take this tiny, thoughtful gift like a good pen or a small tool and wrap it in layers. Small box. Bigger box. Then another. Sometimes duct tape. Sometimes a refrigerator box. Ten minutes of unwrapping, all for something the size of a deck of cards.

But he always laughed. He always kept going. Because the journey became part of the gift. And sometimes I hid something inside the in-between layers just to keep him motivated. That is what breaking down the pile is like. Some parts feel ridiculous. Frustrating. Like, why am I even doing this? But when you get to the core, there is usually something real there. A truth. A tool. A story that still matters. A lie you have believed. A pattern that needed breaking. And the layers were part of getting there. This is not quick work. It is not always clear what is treasure and what is trash, not yet.

During my time teaching, I hit a day when everything felt like too much. I needed to enter grades, make copies, answer emails, and it all felt urgent. Somehow I had no motivation at all. Every free moment I got, I would open my phone, read through emails, or play a game. Anything to avoid doing real work. Then I finally looked around my classroom. Papers were stacked everywhere on my desk, on the counter, on top of books. No wonder I felt buried. So I stopped and said, Let me at least straighten this up. I started sorting the piles. Some papers were trash, some needed filing, and some were just in the wrong place. In a few minutes the physical clutter was gone, and with it most of the stress. Not all of it, but the work heavy feeling lifted almost instantly. That day I remembered something I already knew but had forgotten. Sometimes a clear space makes a clear mind.

Every time you choose to reach for the next layer, to ask What is this really? you lift the weight. You dissolve duplicates. You disarm the cannonballs. You discover that this pile might be a mess, but it might also be a map.

Sticky was not out yet. But he was getting stronger. And for the first time, Sticky was facing his problems.

"The purpose in a man's heart is like deep water, but a man of understanding will draw it out."
Proverbs 20:5

What's Trash and What's Treasure
Sorting the Stuff That Buried You

Once Sticky started really looking at that big old mess, the panic faded. Not because the mess disappeared, but because it was finally in the light. And when you see what you're buried under, you can start to sort it. Not everything you carry is yours. This is the moment things start to change. You're not just getting hit anymore. You're starting to understand what's hitting you.

Some of it needs to be put on a shelf: stories that shaped you, wounds that scarred you but also taught you, wisdom worth keeping. Some of it needs to go in the trash: lies, false identities, guilt that doesn't belong to you, shame you've already outgrown, pressure you were never meant to carry. And some of it? It's harder to place. It feels true, but it might not be true. It feels heavy, but you don't know why. It feels personal, but it didn't start with you.

This is the real work of sorting.

This is where Sticky stopped just surviving the hits and started working through them.

Let's name something clearly: your feelings are never wrong. You feel what you feel, and that's valid. Always. But sometimes the reason you feel that way is a lie you believed somewhere along the way. That's why it's unhelpful when someone says, "You shouldn't feel like that." You already do. The feeling exists. The better question is: "Where is this feeling coming from?"

Sorting the pile means tracing feelings back to their source. And once you know the source, you can decide where it belongs.

A Practical Sorting Tool: "The Three Questions": When you're sitting with something heavy, ask:

1. What happened? (The fact.)
2. What do I believe that means? (The interpretation.)
3. Is that belief true, or just loud? (The test.)

Let me show you what this looks like. I've had the opportunity to counsel some couples, and some of them were struggling badly. One couple in particular could barely communicate without fighting. Everything felt charged. Every word had weight. So we slowed down. I reminded them, "Your feelings aren't wrong. You feel what you feel, and that matters." But then we started identifying the facts: you chose each other. You want good for each other. You're both hurt, but neither of you wants to hurt the other. Then suddenly, the emotions that felt so overwhelming began to reveal their source. They weren't mad because of this moment. They were reacting to old pain, baggage from past relationships, family wounds, trust that had been broken before they met each other. They weren't enemies. They were teammates, fighting the problems, not each other.

And when they finally saw that, it stopped being me versus you and became us versus the problem. That's what sorting does. It gives you clarity. It lets you attach issues to facts, not fears. It doesn't erase the feelings, but it helps you understand where they came from. And once you do that, you can adjust the flow. You can change the story. You don't have to be held hostage by the past.

The Shelf and the Trash

Give yourself two imaginary containers.

The Shelf: for the things you want to remember. Lessons you learned the hard way. Pain you've processed and honored. Memories that still carry truth, even if they hurt. You don't have to relive them, but you don't want to erase them either. This is where your growth goes.

The Trash: for the stuff that no longer belongs. Guilt from someone else's mistake. Expectations that were never realistic. Lies you believed about your worth. You don't need a dramatic ceremony to throw them out. You just need to stop building your identity around them.

Some of the hardest things to sort are the repeat cannonballs, the ones that look new, but are really duplicates of an old, unresolved core issue. Sticky saw this as he kept working. He realized he'd fought the same battle in four different jobs. He'd carried the same fear through three different friendships. He'd felt the same shame since he was a kid, but it wore new clothes every year.

And then one day, he faced it head-on. He named it. He challenged it. He reframed it. And just like that, the other cannonballs that looked just like it started to dissolve. You remember when Sticky picked up that shiny, important-looking ball in the last chapter. He dealt with it, and then saw the sand at his feet. That's what happens when you deal with the core. The duplicates lose their power.

Sorting is holy work. It's slow. Sometimes frustrating. Often emotional. But it's how you heal. Not just by getting rid of the bad stuff, but by finally understanding what you've been carrying all this time.

Sticky didn't finish the pile in a day. But every piece he sorted made space for something better.

From here on, this isn't theory anymore. This is what life starts to look like when you actually do the work.

"Do not be conformed to this world, but be transformed by the renewal of your mind, that by testing you may discern what is the will of God, what is good and acceptable and perfect."
Romans 12:2

The Shelf
Some Things Are Meant to Stay

Sticky was busy sorting the pile, throwing out what didn't belong, old lies, recycled shame, expectations that never fit. But then he came across something that made him stop. It was a moment. A hard one. He picked it up, turned it in his hands, ready to toss it, and then he saw something underneath the pain: growth. Insight. Strength. Sticky didn't go looking for it. He found it by accident. And it wasn't trash. It was proof.

Picture a library, rows and rows of books, sorted by author, sorted by genre: fiction, fantasy, adventure. Non-fiction: cookbooks, psychology, biology, physics. All holding equal weight on the shelves.

Now picture your office, or your room. You have a bookshelf there. It has notebooks with agendas, budgets, maybe a picture of your kids. Mine has a small three-drawer chest I keep pens, pencils, erasers, and markers in. It also has a few knickknacks I've had since I graduated college.

In your kitchen, you have shelves. There's "good" China, for special occasions. And the everyday plates, for making a sandwich when you're in a rush.

That's how the sorting shelf is.

Not everything in the pile is trash. Not everything that hurts needs to be thrown away. Some of it, believe it or not, is treasure. Not shiny treasure. Not a feel-good treasure. But hard-earned, scarred-up, wisdom-soaked treasure. And it doesn't belong in the garbage. It belongs on the shelf.

That's what the shelf is for. It's not where we store random keepsakes or nostalgic junk. It's where we place the truth that shaped us. The reminders. The milestones. The moments that matter. The stories that hurt at first, but healed when we told them again with new eyes.

Here's what goes on the shelf: The time you failed, and got back up. The friendship that ended, but taught you boundaries. The moment you forgave someone who didn't deserve it. The quiet decision to be better than how you were raised. The scar on your heart that proves you survived something you thought might end you.

You don't carry these things every day. You just know where they are. And when life comes back around with a familiar ache or challenge, you look up and see that memory on the shelf and say: "Yeah. I've seen this before. I know who I am."

The shelf gives you identity. Not because it's all pretty, but because it's all true. You've been through some things. And it was not meaningless. It was for you. It made you. That's why it stays.

A client once told me they wanted to "forget everything that happened to them." And I understood the pain behind that wish. But I gently pushed back. "What if you didn't forget it… What if you just stopped carrying it?" Because forgetting is erasing. But placing is honoring. There's a difference between being haunted by the past and learning from it.

The shelf is where the past becomes wisdom, not weight. You want to know something wild? Sometimes the shelf shows us that the worst thing that ever happened to us… ended up building the strongest part of us. That pain you hated? It made you empathetic. That rejection? It taught you discernment. That delay? It built patience you never would've chosen for yourself.

Sticky looked around at the growing shelf in his mind, lined with memories, not as wounds, but as witnesses. Each one is quietly saying: "You've been here before. You didn't quit. You learned something. You became something."

And in the quiet, that shelf became something like confidence.

"Remember the former things, those of long ago; I am God, and there is no other; I am God, and there is none like me."
Isaiah 46:9

The Trash

Letting Go of What Doesn't Serve You Anymore

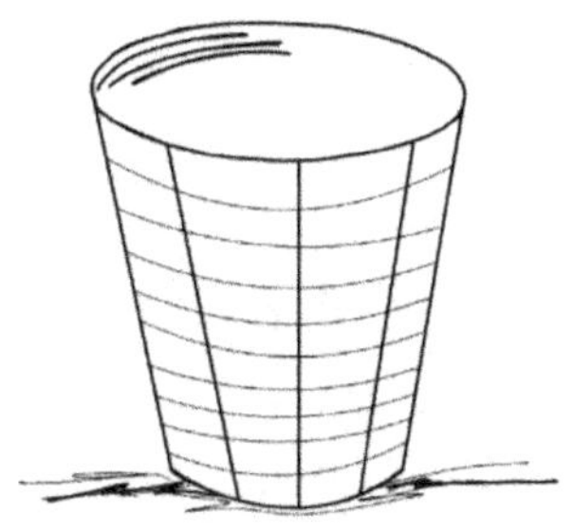

Think about your kitchen trash. Moldy cheese. Scrapings from your toddler's dinner plate. A paper towel soaked in ketchup or coffee. The broken glass and pet hair you swept into the dustpan. You do not throw that stuff away because you hate it. You throw it away because you are done with it.

At a recent event, our hotel was just a short walk from a restaurant we picked for dinner. I wanted to take the long way around and avoid the back alley, but my coworkers insisted on the shortcut behind the hotel's dumpsters. It was everything you would expect, the stink of hundreds of guests' leftovers sitting in the sun and brewing into something almost alive. That is what happens when trash is not dealt with. It does not just sit there. It turns toxic.

The things we throw away used to mean something. That favorite coffee cup you loved for years had value, but once it cracked you let it go. Not out of spite, but because it could not do its job anymore. Guilt, shame, and pressure work the same way. They may have felt necessary at one time, but eventually they start leaking into places they were never meant to reach. We honor the past by learning from it, not by hoarding it.

Sticky had to learn that the hard way. He picked up an old cannonball that looked heavy with meaning. It carried words like loyalty, duty, and self-sacrifice. The longer he held it, the more he realized it was not a gift. It was guilt. It was something that once protected him but had become a prison. He hesitated, almost placed it on the shelf, but then he whispered something that changed everything. "Just because it once served me does not mean it still belongs to me." And he tossed it. Here is the deal. Not everything that helped you survive is going to help you thrive. Some of it was useful for a season. People-pleasing may have kept you from conflict. Shame may have kept you from repeating a mistake. Hustle may have earned approval when love felt out of reach. But now those things are just stink. They take up space in your mind, your marriage, your faith, and your body. The longer they sit, the more they turn into something they were never meant to be.

A Trash Ritual You Can Use

When you find something in your pile that no longer belongs, try this:

1. Name it.

"This is not my responsibility."

"This is a lie I was told."

"This is guilt from a mistake I already made right."

2. Question it.

"Is this still serving me?"

"Is this helping anyone, or just hurting me?"

3. Thank it (optional but healing).

"Thanks for protecting me when I did not know better."

"Thanks for getting me through that season."

"I do not need you anymore."

Toss it. Not in bitterness. In freedom.

Sticky eventually found himself holding several cannonballs that were nothing more than duplicates of an old wound. He had already dealt with the root, but the outer layers kept showing up. He looked at one and, for the first time, really saw it. "I have fought this already." He smiled, dropped it in the trash, and the others began dissolving around him, turning to sand and falling at his feet. What looked like a massive pile had been only echoes of old lies.

I knew exactly how that felt, because I had my own moment like that. I was in a coaching class talking about how I felt bad about how my life had turned out compared to my brothers. I had more joy, more stability, more growth, and I was carrying guilt about it. I told my coach I was comparing my life to theirs. He asked why. I said it was a healthy comparison, something to keep me grounded. He asked again, "Why are you comparing yourself to them?" That is when it hit me. Our choices had nothing to do with each other. The guilt I felt was not humility. It was misplaced. It was trash. So I threw it away. Comparison steals joy. I had been giving it free rent in my soul. As Jordan Peterson says, "Compare yourself to who you were yesterday, not to who someone else is today." I was growing. I was becoming. And I did not need to apologize for it anymore.

Keeping trash does not make you strong. Letting go is strength. You are not a failure for throwing it away. You are finally living like someone who knows their worth.

"Forget the former things, do not dwell on the past. See, I am doing a new thing." Isaiah 43:18–19

INTERMISSION

Sticky's Sorting Guide
Five Questions to Help You Deal With Your Pile

Before life fires again, take a moment to breathe and look at what's been stacked on you. When you're ready, walk each piece through these five questions, slowly and honestly. You don't have to solve everything today, but clarity starts *one question at a time*.

1. Which of these events feel similar enough to group together? Deal with grouped events as one. If they don't belong together, keep them separate.
2. What happened? Name it plainly, just the facts, without commentary or interpretation.
3. What did this make you believe about yourself then, and what does it make you believe about yourself now? This is where identity rises to the surface. Be honest about the story it told you.
4. What's true about it, and what are the lies or leftover feelings you've carried that aren't grounded in truth? Separate what actually happened from the weight you added to it.
5. Does this still serve you or your family in any way, or has it done all it's ever going to do? Some things remain valuable; others have finished their work.

Sorting isn't about rushing; it's about seeing clearly. Sticky learned that every time he answered these questions with honesty, the pile got lighter, his footing stronger, and the next hit didn't bury him the same way. Take your time, you're not behind, and you're not alone. Sticky walked this path, and so can you.

The Return of the Cannon

Life's Still Coming… But You're Not Who You Were

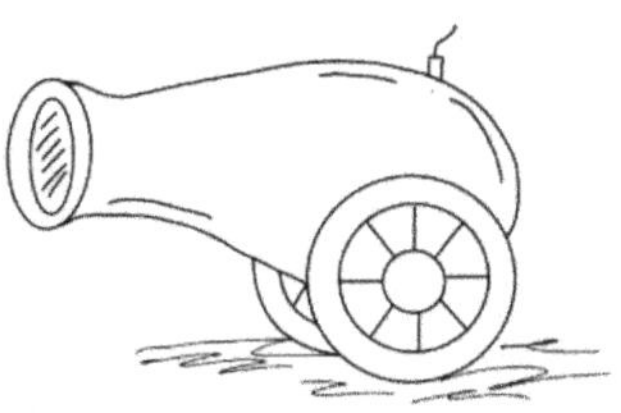

Let's rewind. When Sticky started sorting the pile, unpacking cannonballs, facing what was real, tossing what wasn't, life didn't stop. That's the trap we fall into. We think, "Once I slow down and do the work, everything else will pause too." It doesn't. Life doesn't wait for your breakthroughs. It doesn't check if you have free emotional bandwidth. It just keeps firing, like boom, boom, boom, like it's out of control, lobbing stress and pain and weird relational tension on a loop. Sticky was trying to get his footing, but even as he sorted one mess, another was landing. Then another. Then another.

Eventually, something shifted. The cannon didn't stop, but it started to feel different. The hits were still coming, but Sticky wasn't the same. He could see them sooner. He could read what was coming before it landed. Some he braced for. Some he caught and looked at right away. And some… he didn't even let hit him. He was breaking and sorting them before they ever got close.

The pile wasn't gone. But it wasn't building the same way anymore. That is what growth looks like in real time. You don't flinch at every sound. You stop assuming every problem is yours to hold. You start sorting before you are buried.

Let me be honest with you: I am not quick. It took me a minute to arrive at this. I have made the mistake of thinking I was done. Sorted the pile once, tossed the trash, took a breath, and said, "Okay, I am good now." Then life knocked me down all over again. And I ignored it. And it piled up. Again.

So hear me when I say this. Don't make the same mistake. You will probably get buried again, and that is okay. Just don't stay there. Get back to sorting. Pick up the pieces. Look at each one and ask, Does it teach me? Does it help me? Or is it literally just stuff? And do what you now know how to do.

Sticky picked up a new cannonball and didn't freak out. He rotated it in his hands, checked for labels, then asked the questions: Is this mine? Is this new? Is this just another layer of something I have already faced? He didn't shove it down. He didn't explode. He didn't freeze. He sorted because that is what healed people do.

Growth doesn't make life easier. It just makes you different. You are not reacting anymore. You are responding. You are not building a pile. You are building awareness. Every time you sort one more piece, you get faster. Stronger. Wiser.

Sticky stood in the open, unafraid. The cannonball hit the dirt next to him and rolled to a stop. He smiled. "I have tools. I have space. For the first time, I know what to do."

"Consider it pure joy, whenever you face trials of many kinds, because you know that the testing of your faith produces perseverance."
James 1:2–3

When the Cannonball Is a Wrecking Ball
What to Do When Your System Doesn't Work

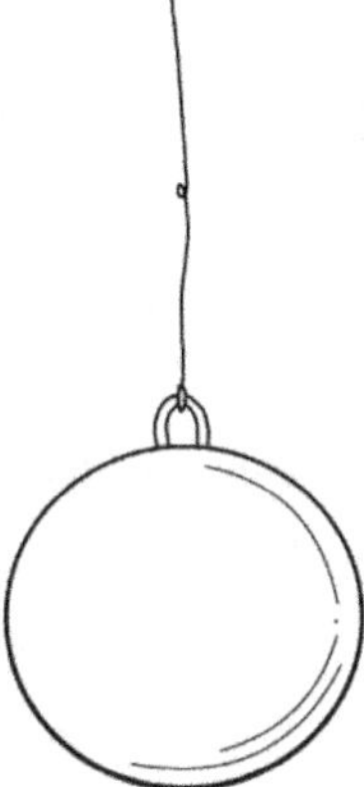

Some hits don't land like the others. They don't bounce, they don't roll, and they don't wait their turn. They hit hard and they change everything. These aren't cannonballs anymore. These are wrecking balls.

Sticky had done the work. He had been sorting, tossing, shelving, and breathing. He knew what to do when life threw junk at him. But then came this. It wasn't a minor pile up or a rough week. It was something deeper, bigger, and heavier. A hit that didn't feel like part of life. It felt like the end of it.

But not every hit fits inside the system. Some moments don't feel like something to sort. They feel like something that changes everything. On September 9, 2012, my brothers and I sat in a little room at the hospital. The doctor told us our mom wasn't going to recover and that her quality of life would never return. We were faced with the impossible decision to take her off life support and see if she could fight on her own. Less than two hours later, she was gone. I remember sitting there in shock, hearing nurses give condolences, listening to questions I wasn't really processing. We went home. I crawled into bed with my young son as he napped and just sobbed.

I don't remember anything else about September. Nothing. I know I had a birthday. I know I taught a class. I know we had dinner and guests and church. I even spoke at her funeral. But that whole month is blank. Grief does that. It doesn't just hit you, it levels you. And even though, with time, we found a new rhythm, I was never the same again. There was life before that moment and life after it.

Another moment came in 2006. It was a different kind of hit, but the same kind of shift. A hurricane was bearing down and we fled in the night. Gas lines were two hours long. We packed what we could and headed for my in-laws. We stayed there for two weeks. Schools closed and streets flooded. Life paused, but it didn't actually stop. Bills still came. Kids still needed dinner. And slowly, the storm passed, cleanup began, and we moved forward. That moment carved a line through our story. There was a before and an after.

So what do you do when the system doesn't work, when your pile sorting tools aren't enough, when everything is leveled and your heart is offline? You don't fix it. You don't label it. You don't pretend to be okay. You feel it. You give it space. You let the wreckage be real. Sticky sat in the ruins. Not defeated, just human. His tools were somewhere under the rubble and he didn't move for a while. He wasn't ready to. And that was okay. Some pain doesn't get sorted on day one. Some wounds don't heal with clarity. They heal with time, support, and gentleness. When the hit is big enough, even healing has to sit still. Here is what I have learned: You don't have to explain your wrecking ball to anyone. You don't have to apologize for how much it hurt. And you don't have to rush back to the process. You will get back there, but today might only be about breathing, crying, or sitting still in your son's bed holding a pillow and letting it fall apart for a little while. And that is not failure. That is grief. That is honoring what you have lost.

"The Lord is close to the brokenhearted and saves those who are crushed in spirit."
Psalm 34:18

When You Miss One
The Quiet Crash of Complacency

Sticky had done the work. He sorted his pile. He shelved the meaningful stuff. He threw out the garbage. He moved forward like someone who had learned the lessons. And then he missed one. It was not a wrecking ball. It was not even a big cannonball. Just a normal one, the kind he thought he had handled by now. He did not catch it or even see it coming. He was too comfortable, a little too confident. "I have got this," he thought. "I do not have to watch as closely anymore." "This part of me is fixed."

I know the feeling. I stood on the edge of something new, and not just a cleaned-up room or a better schedule. I was untangling real-life junk: debt, broken relationships, and patterns that had haunted me for years. I cut ties with drama. I paid off the card that never seemed to go away. I started showing up, keeping my word, tightening the bolts of my day-to-day. And it felt good, like breathing fresh air after years underground.

I even said it out loud: "That is it. No more self-sabotage. No more old me." I pictured this wise, focused, grounded version of myself, like a coach watching the game from the sideline, calm and in control. And for a while, I lived like him. I budgeted. I planned. I said no when I needed to. I woke up early. I started feeling like someone new.

But somewhere in that rhythm, I relaxed a little too much. It started small. One little splurge. "This email can wait." "That promise? I will follow through next week." Then I was skipping calls. Deadlines piled up. I started dodging things again, numbing out a little at a time. I watched, almost in slow motion, as my clean calendar turned into chaos. That small indulgence put me back in debt. That rescheduled meeting disappointed a client. That ignored text became a crisis. It was me all over again, and not because I did not know better, but because I stopped watching.

That is the danger of healing. It can make you think you have arrived, that the system runs itself now. But it does not.

Sticky looked at the mess and knew exactly what happened. He had not exploded. He had not collapsed. He had just let go of the discipline. He assumed the work was over. But missing one does not erase your progress. It simply means it is time to start sorting again. So that is what he did, and what I did. Not with shame. Not with panic. Just honesty and grace.

You are going to miss one. Maybe more than one. You are going to feel like you should be past this by now. But healing is not linear. You do not graduate from being human. So next time, catch it sooner. Sort it faster. And remember that every time you get up, it takes a little less time to rebuild.

Keep Going, you will miss one. You will slip, fall behind, and let something slide. But you are not who you used to be. That is the part we overlook in the mess. You have grown. You are not starting over. You are starting again from higher ground.

That moment you caught yourself and said, "I cannot let this pile up again"? That is proof. You have built something. You have learned something. You have become someone. Growth does not always feel big. Sometimes it is quiet. It looks like breathing instead of reacting, pausing instead of panicking, choosing grace instead of shame. Celebrate that. Even small steps forward count, especially when you are tired and especially when you used to give up. So do not panic

when you slip. Do not shame yourself when you stall. Just refocus.
Take one small step. And keep going. Growth is not about never
missing a step. It is about not staying stuck.
That is how Sticky moved forward. That is how you move forward.
Not perfectly, but steadily.

"Let us not become weary in doing good, for at the proper time we will reap a harvest if we do not give up."
Galatians 6:9

Sticky Helps Someone Else
Healing turns outward

Sticky was moving around in his own little world, minding his own business, when something caught his eye: a pile that wasn't his. Some of the stuff looked familiar, but it wasn't his. Then he noticed a hand reaching out from a gap in the pile.

At some point, your story stops being only about you. You've been through the pile. You've learned to sort. You have faced your own stuff, thrown out what no longer belonged, and honored what needed to stay. You have grown. And then one day, someone crosses your path who is buried under their own weight, covered in silence and strain, eyes barely visible through the rubble. A hand reaches out, and this time, you are the one who sees it. Sticky was born for moments like that, but the truth is, so was I.

When I was working as a high-risk coordinator, students came to my office for a hundred different reasons. Grades. Suspensions. Conflicts. Nothing about the job description prepared me for the handful who walked in carrying something far heavier. These were not kids worried about algebra or friend drama. These were kids whose lives were on the line. Kids who felt the kind of pressure where "quit" did not mean quitting a class or quitting a team. It meant the kind of quit you do not come back from. The quiet kind that slips in when the pain feels permanent.

The first time it happened, I felt the bottom drop out of my stomach. My mouth went dry. My words scattered. I felt entirely unqualified to help, unsure what to say, and afraid that one wrong word might push them further toward the edge. They never said the exact phrase that would require emergency protocol, but everything about their posture said they were close, maybe closer than they even knew how to articulate. And there I was, sitting across the desk, a grown man with a pen and a notepad, trying to steady my own heartbeat long enough to steady theirs.

I remember thinking, "I cannot say 'Please don't kill yourself,'" because they would shut down or bolt out the door. Yet saying nothing felt even more dangerous. I was not an expert. I had not counseled someone through that level of despair before. Yes, I had lost a friend years earlier, but I only understood it from a distance. Now I was face to face with a hurting teenager who felt like they had reached the last stop on the train. So I reached for what I had. Literally. A pen. A notepad. And a tiny stick figure named Sticky. I drew the cannon firing. I drew Sticky trying to block the hits. I drew the pile building. I drew the choices underneath, the same ones you have seen. Explode. Quit. And I watched that student study the drawing, eyes fixed on the word "quit." They understood the meaning without me needing to spell it out. They knew what it represented.

Then I drew the third option. Examine. Sort. Decide what stays and what goes. And somehow, this simple sketch helped them see themselves more clearly than any speech I could have given. I drew the trash can. I drew the shelf. And something shifted in the room. They realized they were not out of choices after all. The pile was heavy, but it was not permanent. There was more to do than just collapse or disappear. There was another way.

And something shifted in me too. I was scared to speak. Scared I would fail them. Scared I would not be enough. But sitting there with that notepad between us, I understood something I had never seen so clearly until that moment. You do not have to be perfect to help someone. You do not need all the answers. You just have to be honest. Present. Real. You have to offer what you have, even if you worry it is not enough.

Your scars can light someone else's path, not because your pain was noble or pretty, but because you survived it. That day, Sticky helped that student, but I helped them too. Because I had been buried and found a way to get back up. And now they could too.

Sticky saw that hand sticking out of the pile, and he calmly reached for it. He didn't pull them out. He just let them know he was there. He helped them sit up. Helped them see what they were under. Healing turns outward when you least expect it. Not to build a platform. Not to pretend you have arrived. But to help someone else feel less alone. To remind them there is still a way forward. That there is still a third choice.

"Praise be to the God and Father of our Lord Jesus Christ, the Father of compassion and the God of all comfort, who comforts us in all our troubles, so that we can comfort those in any trouble with the comfort we ourselves receive from God."
2 Corinthians 1:3–4

You're Still Gonna Get Hit

The cannon doesn't stop, but now you know what to do.

Sticky had sorted the pile. He'd made peace with his past. He'd found purpose in the pain. And life was better. But the cannon never shut off. It just changed rhythm.

The hits kept coming. Not always heavy, not always life-shattering. But steady. Quiet ones. Random ones. The kind that tests your mood, not your survival. And Sticky still got hit. But now, he knew how to respond.

This is the part no one wants to say out loud: it doesn't end. There's no final level where life chills out and nothing bothers you. Even when you're healthy. Even when you're helping others. Even when you've done all the work, you're still gonna get hit.

But now you don't fall apart. You recognize the pattern. You know what to do. You catch it quicker, or if you miss one, you sort it out before it buries you. That's what maturity looks like. Not perfection, but resilience.

I'm reminded of a trip with my family. We were headed to the beach on an eight-hour drive. We were two hours from the destination, everyone was a little tired, a little cranky, and then, flat tire. Okay! We've got a spare. But the tire had a locking lug, and we didn't have the tool. It was hot. The kids were grumpy. We were stuck on the side of the road. No big deal. We made a call, got towed, the garage got the lug off, changed the tire, and two hours later we were back on track. We laughed. The kids actually made the most of it. It became a moment, not a meltdown.

Years ago, a moment like that would have wrecked me. I would've snapped, blamed someone, let the whole day spiral. But standing on the side of that highway, I felt something different. A deep breath. A steadiness that wasn't there in my twenties or thirties. I realized anger had nothing helpful to offer, and this wasn't a dead end, just a detour. We were still going to the beach. Life wasn't falling apart. It was simply asking me to handle an inconvenience with grace instead of panic. And for the first time, I actually could.

Because I'd been through worse. Because I'd learned to breathe, not break. I wasn't buried, I was just inconvenienced.

That's what happens after the pile. Sticky had become someone who could take a hit without unraveling. And so have you.

You'll still get flat tires, still get bad news, still get frustrated. But now you catch it quicker. You respond instead of react. You keep your footing.

This is what the work has led to: you know your tools. You sort things before they bury you. You can even help someone else while you're getting hit yourself. You're not broken. You're growing. And this is what grown looks like.

"Therefore, put on the full armor of God, so that when the day of evil comes, you may be able to stand your ground, and after you have done everything, to stand."
Ephesians 6:13

So What Now?

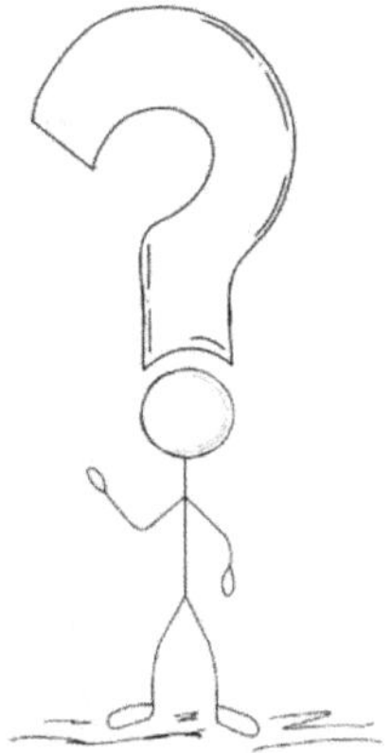

Sticky still gets hit. Not every shot is heavy. Some sting. Some surprise him. Some hurt worse than expected. But he does not panic anymore. He catches what he can. Sorts what he needs. Shelves the good. Trashes the stuff that doesn't help. And when one slips through, he does not spiral. He resets.

That is what this journey has built. You have done the work. You faced the pile. You did not explode. You did not quit. You sorted, you learned, you grew. And you are still here. That matters. That is real. That is not a soft kind of strong. It is the kind of strong that bends without breaking.

He was at the grocery store. Sticky, older now, a little slower, a little wiser, stood in line behind a man fumbling through his pockets, trying to pay. His face was flushed and his card declined. There was frustration in his voice. Others behind them started sighing. Sticky stepped forward and said, "I got you, man. No problem. Have a great day." He paid the bill and kept moving. He had been there. The card declined. People are staring. It stinks.

The man mumbled something and rushed off. Sticky bagged his groceries, walked out, and did not overthink it. A few years ago, he might have gotten annoyed, judged, or avoided. Now he just saw someone buried, and he had a little extra room in his hands. It was not that much, and he was down to help someone when and where he could.

It reminded me of something that happened on a trip with my boys. We were supposed to fly to Maryland, pick up my older son, and road-trip home together. Flights were booked and the plan was tight.

We left the house at four thirty in the morning. It should have been smooth. Until we got a flat tire with no spare. My wife jumped in the truck to help. My younger son called an Uber. We scrambled, regrouped, and somehow made it to the airport.

At the counter, my son checked the screenshot I sent him. Gate three. We went to gate three. No flight. We looked again and it was gate twelve. We sprinted across the airport and arrived just in time to watch the gate agent close the door. We missed it.

We booked a later flight and waited it out. After landing in Washington D.C., we headed to the rental counter, only to find out they were behind because of the government shutdown. Delays everywhere. Then the real punch. "You used a debit card. We cannot do a one-way rental with a debit card." Every part of the plan evaporated. The bank locked my card for fraud because I tried too many times.

So we ordered an Uber to my son's place. I sat there stewing, frustrated, embarrassed, wanting so badly for the plan to work. Then I looked at my boys. They were relaxed. Laughing. Enjoying the moment. And it hit me that the perfect plan did not matter. They just wanted to be with me.

So we shifted. We explored the capital. Went to the zoo. Played games. Ate food. Walked together and talked together. It was not the plan. It was better. Somewhere in all of it, I had to admit that this was not my plan. This was God's plan. I tried to orchestrate everything and God said, "You do not need a perfect trip. You need time with your boys." That moment revealed something I did not expect. I had grown. I did not break when the plan fell apart. I had learned to breathe, not panic.

I had learned to adapt.

That is what healing looks like on an ordinary day.

Sticky reminds me of a grandpa. Not because of age, but because of that quiet calm. The kind of presence that does not flinch when life hits. He has been through enough to know this will not be the end of him. Even if he does not know exactly what to do, he knows not to panic.

That is what you are stepping into. Not a perfect life. Not a flawless system. But a deeper, quieter confidence.

And me? I still hurt. I still do not always understand. Sometimes the unknown still rattles me. But I have fought enough piles to know there is a way forward. And now you do too.

We cannot stop the cannon. But we can face it differently now. With honesty. With wisdom. With each other. You and I can do this together.

"Consider it pure joy, my brothers and sisters, whenever you face trials of many kinds, because you know that the testing of your faith produces perseverance."
James 1:2–3

This is the end of the book. But not the end of you. Keep going. Keep sorting. Keep standing.

Before you move on, don't just close this book and say, "That was good."

Pick one thing. Just one. Something small. Something recent. Something you've been avoiding. Walk it through the questions: What happened? What did it make you believe? Is that actually true? Don't try to fix your whole life today. That's how the pile builds again. Just deal with one piece. That's where this starts.

Not tomorrow. Not when things slow down. **Right here.**